WORDS TO
WINNERS OF SOULS

WORDS TO
WINNERS OF SOULS

Horatius Bonar

P U B L I S H I N G
P.O. BOX 817 • PHILLIPSBURG • NEW JERSEY 08865-0817

Newly typeset edition, 1995
by
Presbyterian and Reformed Publishing Company
Phillipsburg, New Jersey
and
the den Dulk Foundation
Hanford, California

Library of Congress Cataloging-in-Publication-Data

Bonar, Horatius, 1808–1889
    Words to winners of souls / Horatius Bonar.
        p.   cm.
    Originally published: Boston : American Tract Society,
1860.
    ISBN-10: 0-87552-164-9
    ISBN-13: 978-0-87552-164-0
    1. Pastoral theology—Early works to 1900. I. Title.
BV4010.B6 1995
253—dc10   94–43442

CONTENTS

Preface   vii

I

Importance of a Living Ministry   1

II

The Minister's True Life and Walk   9

III

Past Defects   17

IV

Ministerial Confession   25

V

Revival in the Ministry   49

Preface

IT IS NOT DIFFICULT to write a preface to this classic treasure of the Christian ministry written by a Scottish Presbyterian divine who was born in Edinburgh on December 19, 1808, and died there on July 31, 1889. He belongs to a previous generation, but his little manual is timeless, for it fits into the needs of our day almost as accurately as it did into the needs of the parish of Kelso in 1866 and later in Edinburgh.

Horatius Bonar was first of all a "winner of souls," although he was also a great preacher and a writer of some of our best hymns. He became Moderator of the General Assembly of his Church.

When we read his manual on how to win men for Christ, we are reminded, page after page, of his three best hymns, although he was the author of many. He could say, himself, "I heard the voice of Jesus say," and therefore he could write the hymn beginning with those words.

How many have been led to Christ by this invitation to accept Him as their Savior, and how many Christians have rededicated themselves to their Lord and Master and have recalled the day when they first loved Him, when they have sung at the Holy Communion, "Here, O my Lord, I See Thee Face to Face"!

Not only are his counsels to the winners of souls spiritual, divine and searching, but the keynote of it all is that of urgency, as he himself expressed it in his third great hymn, "Go Labor On, Spend and Be Spent." The third stanza of that hymn ought to be written as a motto on the desk of every pastor:

> "Go, labor on while it is day,
>   The world's dark night is hastening on.
> Speed, speed thy work, cast sloth away—
>   It is not thus that souls are won."

This is a book for winners of souls, not for loiterers on the highway or for slothful servants of our Master. It is a heart-searching book, but also one that gives new courage to continue the daily task. Reprinted again and again by the American Tract Society, it is now issued by request in slightly abridged form.

There are two books that tell the story of Horatius Bonar's life in detail. One is entitled, *Horatius Bonar, a Memorial*, published in 1899, and the other is *Memories of Dr. Horatius Bonar, by Relatives and Public Men*, (Edinburgh, 1909). Both have a portrait as frontispiece.

I recall as a boy one little book that used to lie on my father's desk—that is sixty years ago—in his pastoral study in Michigan. It was his constant companion and was marked almost on every page. This little volume, bound in leather with gilt edges, had on the cover, *Words to Winners of Souls*.

Samuel M. Zwemer, D.D.
1867-1952

New York City
March 3, 1950

" 'Tis not for man to trifle. Life is brief,
    And sin is here.
Our age is but the falling of a leaf—
    A dropping tear.
We have no time to sport away the hours:
All must be earnest in a world like ours.

"Not *many* lives, but only *one* have we,—
    One, only one;
How sacred should that one life ever be
    That narrow span!
Day after day filled up with blessed toil,
Hour after hour still bringing in new spoil."

I

Importance of a Living Ministry

"How much more would a few good and fervent men effect in the ministry than a multitude of lukewarm ones!" said Oecolampadius, the Swiss Reformer—a man who had been taught by experience, and who has recorded that experience for the benefit of other churches and other days.

The mere multiplying of men calling themselves ministers of Christ will avail little. They may be but "cumberers of the ground." They may be like Achan, troubling the camp; or perhaps Jonah, raising the tempest. Even when sound in the faith, through unbelief, lukewarmness and slothful formality, they may do irreparable injury to the cause of Christ, freezing and withering up all spiritual life around them. The lukewarm ministry of one who is theoretically orthodox is often more extensively and fatally ruinous to souls than that of one grossly inconsistent or flagrantly heretical. "What man on earth is so pernicious a drone as an idle minister?" said Cecil. And Fletcher remarked well that "lukewarm pastors made careless Christians." Can the multiplication of such ministers, to whatever amount, be counted a blessing to a people?

When the church of Christ, in all her denominations, returns to primitive example, and walking in apostolical footsteps seeks to be conformed more closely to inspired models, allowing nothing that pertains to earth to come between her and her living Head, then will she give more careful heed to see that the men to whom she entrusts the care of souls, however learned and able, should be yet more distinguished by their spirituality, zeal, faith and love.

In comparing Baxter and Orton, the biographer of the former remarks that "Baxter would have set the world on fire while Orton was lighting a match." How true! Yet not true alone of Baxter or of Orton. These two individuals are representatives of two classes in the church of Christ in every age and of every denomination. The latter class are far the more numerous: the Ortons you may count by hundreds, the Baxters by tens; yet who would not prefer a solitary specimen of the one to a thousand of the other?

Baxter's Burning Sincerity

"When he spoke of weighty soul concerns," says one of his contemporaries of Baxter, "you *might find his very spirit drenched therein."* No wonder that he was blessed with such amazing success! Men felt that in listening to him they were in contact with one who was dealing with realities of infinite moment.

This is one of the secrets of ministerial strength and ministerial success. And who can say how much of the overflowing infidelity of the present day is owing not only to the lack of spiritual instructors—not merely to the existence of grossly unfaithful and inconsistent ones—but to the *coldness* of many who are reputed sound and faithful. Men cannot but feel that if religion is worth anything, it is worth everything; that if it calls for any measure of zeal and warmth, it will justify the utmost degrees of these; and that there is no consistent medium between reckless atheism and the intensest warmth of religious zeal. Men may dislike, detest, scoff at, persecute the latter, yet their consciences are all the while silently reminding them that if there be a God and a Savior, a heaven and a hell, anything short of such life and love is hypocrisy, dishonesty, perjury!

And thus the lesson they learn from the lifeless discourses of the class we are alluding to is, that, since these men do not believe the doctrines they are preaching, there is no need of their hearers believing them; if ministers only believe them because they make their living by them, why should those who make nothing by them scruple about denying them?

"*Rash* preaching," said Rowland Hill, "disgusts; *timid* preaching leaves poor souls fast asleep; *bold* preaching is the only preaching that is owned of God."

It is not merely unsoundness in faith, or negligence

in duty, or open inconsistency of life that mars the ministerial work and ruins souls. A man may be free from all scandal either in creed or conduct, and yet may be a most grievous obstruction in the way of all spiritual good to his people. He may be a dry and empty cistern, notwithstanding his orthodoxy. He may be freezing or blasting life at the very time he is speaking of the way of life. He may be repelling men from the cross even when he is in words proclaiming it. He may be standing between his flock and the blessing even when he is, in outward form, lifting up his hand to bless them. The same words that from warm lips would drop as the rain, or distill as the dew, fall from his lips as the snow or hail, chilling all spiritual warmth and blighting all spiritual life. How many souls have been lost for want of earnestness, want of solemnity, want of love in the preacher, even when the words uttered were precious and true!

Our One Object: to Win Souls

We take for granted that the object of the Christian ministry *is to convert sinners and to edify the body of Christ.* No faithful minister can possibly rest short of this. Applause, fame, popularity, honor, wealth—all these are vain. If souls are not won, if saints are not matured, our ministry itself is vain.

The question, therefore, which each of us has to answer to his own conscience is, "Has it been the end of my ministry, has it been the desire of my heart to save the lost and guide the saved? Is this my aim in *every sermon* I preach, in every visit I pay? Is it under the influence of this feeling that I continually live and walk and speak? Is it for this I pray and toil and fast and weep? Is it for this I spend and am spent, counting it, next to the salvation of my own soul, my chiefest joy to be the instrument of saving others? Is it for this that I exist? To accomplish this would I gladly die? Have I seen the pleasure of the Lord prospering in my hand? Have I seen souls converted under my ministry? Have God's people found refreshment from my lips and gone upon their way rejoicing, or have I seen no fruit of my labors, and yet am content to remain unblest? Am I satisfied to preach, and yet not know of one saving impression made, one sinner awakened?"

Nothing short of positive success can satisfy a true minister of Christ. His plans may proceed smoothly and his external machinery may work steadily, but without actual fruit in the saving of souls he counts all these as nothing. His feeling is: *"My little children, of whom I travail in birth again until Christ be formed in you"* (Galatians 4:19). And it is this feeling which makes him successful.

"Ministers," said Owen, "are seldom honored with success unless they are continually aiming at the conversion of sinners." The resolution that in the strength and with the blessing of God he will never rest without success, will insure it. It is the man who has made up his mind to confront every difficulty, who has counted the cost and, fixing his eye upon the prize, has determined to fight his way to it—it is such a man that conquers.

The dull apathy of other days is gone. Satan has taken the field actively, and it is best to meet him front

5

to front. Besides, men's consciences are really on edge. God seems extensively striving with them, as before the flood. A breath of the Divine Spirit has passed over the earth, and hence the momentous character of the time, as well as the necessity for improving it so long as it lasts.*

The one true goal or resting-place where doubt and weariness, the stings of a pricking conscience, and the longings of an unsatisfied soul would all be quieted, is *Christ Himself*. Not the church, but Christ. Not doctrine, but Christ. Not forms, but Christ. Not ceremonies, but Christ; Christ the God-man, giving His life for ours; sealing the everlasting covenant, and making peace for us through the blood of His cross; Christ the divine storehouse of all light and truth, *"In whom are hid all the treasures of wisdom and knowledge"* (Colossians 2:3); Christ the infinite vessel, filled with the Holy Spirit, the Enlightener, the Teacher, the Quickener, the Comforter, so that *"of his fullness have all we received, and grace for grace"* (John 1:16). This, this alone is the vexed soul's refuge, its rock to build on, its home to abide in till the great tempter be bound and every conflict ended in victory.

Meet "Opinion" With the Truth

Let us, then, meet this "earnestness" which is now the boast, but may ere long be the bane, of the age, with

---

* Bonar's comments on spiritual conditions in his day (1859) are strikingly appropriate for the present.

that which alone can bring down its feverish pulse, and soothe it into blessed calm, the gospel of the grace of God. All other things are but opiates, drugs, quackeries; this is the divine medicine; this is the sole, the speedy, the eternal cure. It is not by "opinion" that we are to meet "opinion"; it is the *Truth of God* that we are to wield; and applying the *edge* of the "sword of the Spirit" to the theories of man (which he proudly calls his "opinions"), make him feel what a web of sophistry and folly he has been weaving for his own entanglement and ruin.

It is not opinions that man needs: it is *Truth*. It is not theology: it is *God*. It is not religion: it is *Christ*. It is not literature and science; but the knowledge of the free love of God in the gift of His only-begotten Son.

"I know not," says Richard Baxter, "what others think, but for my own part I am ashamed of my stupidity, and wonder at myself that I deal not with my own and others' souls as one that looks for the great day of the Lord; and that I can have room for almost any other thoughts and words; and that such astonishing matters do not wholly absorb my mind. I marvel how I can preach of them slightly and coldly; and how I can let men alone in their sins; and that I do not go to them, and beseech them, for the Lord's sake, to repent, however they may take it, and whatever pain and trouble it should cost me.

"I seldom come out of the pulpit but my conscience smiteth me that I have been no more serious and fervent. It accuseth me not so much for want of ornaments and elegancy, nor for letting fall an unhandsome word; but it asketh me, 'How couldst thou speak of life and death with such a heart? How couldst thou preach of heaven and hell in such a careless, sleepy manner? Dost thou believe what thou sayest? Art thou in earnest, or in jest? How canst thou tell people that sin is such a thing, and that so much misery is upon them and before them, and be no more affected with it? Shouldst thou not weep over such a people, and should not thy tears interrupt thy words? Shouldst thou not cry aloud, and show them their transgressions; and entreat and beseech them as for life and death?'

"Truly this is the peal that conscience doth ring in my ears, and yet my drowsy soul will not be awakened. Oh, what a thing is an insensible, hardened heart! O Lord, save us from the plague of infidelity and hardheartedness ourselves, or else how shall we be fit instruments of saving others from it? Oh, do that on our souls which thou wouldst use us to do on the souls of others!"

II

The Minister's True Life and Walk

THE TRUE MINISTER must be a *true* Christian. He must be called by God before he can call others to God. The Apostle Paul thus states the matter: "*God . . . hath reconciled us to himself by Jesus Christ, and hath given to us the ministry of reconciliation*" (2 Corinthians 5:18). They were first reconciled, and then they had given to them the ministry of reconciliation. Are we *ministers* reconciled? It is but reasonable that a man who is to act as a spiritual guide to others should himself know the way of salvation. It has been frequently said that "the way to heaven is blocked up with dead professors"; but is it not true also that the melancholy obstruction is not composed of *members* of churches only? Let us take heed unto ourselves!

As the minister's life is in more than one respect the life of a ministry, let us speak a few words on ministerial holy living.

Let us seek the Lord *early*. "If my heart be early seasoned with his presence, it will savor of him all day after." Let us see God before man every day. "I ought to pray before seeing any one. Often when I sleep long, or meet with others early, and then have family prayer and breakfast and forenoon callers, it is eleven or twelve o'clock before I begin secret prayer. This is a wretched system. It is unscriptural. Christ rose before day, and went into a solitary place. . . . Family prayer loses much of power and sweetness, and I can do no good to those who come to seek for me. The conscience feels guilty, the soul unfed, the lamp not trimmed. Then, when secret prayer comes, the soul is often out of tune. I feel it far better to begin with God, to see His face first, to get my soul near Him before it is near another. . . . It is best to have at least one hour *alone with God* before engaging in anything else. At the same time, I must be careful not to reckon communion with God by minutes or hours, or by solitude." (McCheyne)

Hear this true servant of Christ exhorting a beloved brother: "Take heed to *thyself*. Your own soul is your first and greatest care. You know a sound body alone can work with power, much more a *healthy soul*. Keep a clear conscience through the blood of the Lamb. Keep up close communion with God. Study likeness to Him in all things. Read the Bible for your own growth first, then for your people."

"With him," says his biographer, "the commencement of all labor invariably consisted in the preparation of his own soul. The forerunner of each day's visitations was a calm season of private devotion during morning

10

hours. The walls of his chamber were witnesses of his prayerfulness—I believe of his tears as well as of his cries. The pleasant sound of psalms often issued from his room at an early hour; then followed the reading of the Word for his own sanctification: and few have so fully realized the blessing of the first psalm." Would that it were so with us all! "Devotion," said Bishop Hall, "is the life of religion, the very soul of piety, the highest employment of grace." It is much to be feared that "we are weak in the pulpit because we are weak in the closet."

"Walking With God"

"To restore a commonplace truth," writes Mr. Coleridge, "to its first uncommon luster, you need only translate it into action." *Walking with God* is a very commonplace truth. Translate this truth into action—how lustrous it becomes! The phrase, how hackneyed!—the thing, how rare! It is such a walk—not an abstract ideal, but a personality, a life—which the reader is invited to contemplate. Oh, that we would only set ourselves in right earnest to this rare work of translation!

It is said of the energetic, pious and successful John Berridge that "communion with God was what he enforced in the latter stages of his ministry. It was, indeed, his own meat and drink, and the banquet from which he never appeared to rise." This shows us the source of his great strength. If we were always sitting at this banquet, then it might be recorded of us ere long, as of him, "He was in the first year visited by about a thousand persons under serious impressions."

Study the Speakers, Not the Sermons

To the *men* even more than to their doctrine we would point the eye of the inquirer who asks, Whence came their success? Why, may not the same success be ours? We may take the sermons of Whitefield or Berridge or Edwards for our study or our pattern, but it is the individuals themselves that we must mainly set before us; it is with the spirit of the men, more than of their works, that we are to be imbued, if we are emulous of a ministry as powerful, as victorious as theirs. They were spiritual men, and walked with God. It is living fellowship with a living Savior which, transforming us into His image, fits us for being able and successful ministers of the gospel.

Without this nothing else will avail. Neither orthodoxy, nor learning, nor eloquence, nor power of argument, nor zeal, nor fervor, will accomplish naught without this. It is this that gives power to our words and persuasiveness to our arguments, making them either as the balm of Gilead to the wounded spirit or as sharp arrows of the mighty to the conscience of the stouthearted rebel. From them that walk with Him in holy, happy intercourse, a virtue seems to go forth, a blessed fragrance seems to compass them whithersoever they go. Nearness to Him, intimacy with Him, assimilation to His character—these are the elements of a ministry of power.

When we can tell our people, "We beheld His glory, and therefore we speak of it; it is not from report we speak, but we have *seen* the King in His beauty"— how lofty the position we occupy! Our power in drawing men to Christ springs chiefly from the fullness of our personal joy in Him, and the nearness of our personal communion with Him. The countenance that reflects most of Christ, and shines most with His love and grace, is most fitted to attract the gaze of a careless, giddy world, and win restless souls from the fascinations of creature love and creature-beauty. A ministry of power must be the fruit of a holy, peaceful, loving intimacy with the Lord.

Faithfulness Essential to Success

"The law of truth was in his mouth, and iniquity was not found in his lips: he walked with me in peace and equity, and did turn many away from iniquity" (Malachi 2:6). Let us observe the connection here declared to subsist between faithfulness and success in the work of the ministry; between a godly life and the "turning away many from iniquity." The end for which we first took office, as we declared at ordination, was the *saving of souls;* the end for which we still live and labor is the same; the means to this end are a holy life and a faithful fulfillment of our ministry.

The connection between these two things is close and sure. We are entitled to calculate upon it. We are called upon to pray and labor with the confident expectation of its being realized; and where it is not, to examine ourselves with all diligence, lest the cause of the failure be found in ourselves; in our want of faith, love, prayer, zeal and warmth, spirituality and holiness of life; for it is by these that the Holy Spirit is grieved away. Success is attainable; success is desirable; success is promised by God; and nothing on earth can be more bitter to the soul of a faithful minister than the want of it. To walk with God, and to be faithful to our trust, is declared to be the certain way of attaining it. Oh, how much depends on the holiness of our life, the consistency of our character, the heavenliness of our walk and conversation!

Our position is such that we cannot remain neutral. Our life cannot be one of harmless obscurity. We must either repel or attract—save or ruin souls! How loud, then, the call, how strong the motive, to spirituality of soul and circumspectness of life! How solemn the warning against worldly-mindedness and vanity, against levity and frivolity, against negligence, sloth and cold formality!

Of all men, a minister of Christ is especially called to walk with God. Everything depends on this; his own peace and joy, his own future reward at the coming of the Lord. But especially does God point to this as the true and sure way of securing the blessing. This is the grand secret of ministerial success. One who walks with God reflects the light of His countenance upon a benighted world; and the closer he walks, the more of this light does he reflect. One who walks with God carries in his very air and countenance a sweet serenity and holy joy that

14

diffuses tranquillity around. One who walks with God receives and imparts life whithersoever he goes; as it is written, out of him *"shall flow rivers of living water"* (John 7:38). He is not merely the world's light but the world's fountain, dispensing the water of life on every side and making the barren waste to blossom as the rose. He waters the world's wilderness as he moves along his peaceful course. His life is blessed; his example is blessed; his intercourse is blessed; his words are blessed; his ministry is blessed! Souls are saved, sinners are converted, and many are turned from their iniquity.

III

PAST DEFECTS

"O my God, I am ashamed and blush to lift up my face to thee, my God . . . O our God, what shall we say after this?"—EZRA 9:6, 10.

To DELIVER SERMONS on each returning Lord's Day, to administer the Lord's Supper stately, to pay an occasional visit to those who request it, to attend religious meetings—this, we fear, sums up the ministerial life of multitudes who are, by profession, overseers of the flock of Christ. An incumbency of thirty, forty or fifty years often yields no more than this. So many sermons, so many baptisms, so many sacraments, so many visits, so many meetings of various kinds—these are all the pastoral annals, the parish records, the ALL of a lifetime's ministry to many! Of *souls* that have been saved, such a record could make no mention.

17

Multitudes have perished under such a ministry; the judgment only will disclose whether so much as one has been saved. There might be learning, but there was no "tongue of the learned to speak a word in season to him that is weary." There might be wisdom, but it certainly was not the wisdom that "winneth souls." There might even be the sound of the gospel, but it seemed to contain no glad tidings at all; it was not sounded forth from warm lips into startled ears as the message of eternal life, "the glorious gospel of the blessed God." Men lived, and it was never asked of them by their minister whether they were born again! Men sickened, sent for the minister and received a prayer upon their deathbeds as their passport into heaven. Men died, and were buried where all their fathers had been laid; there was a prayer at their funeral, and decent respects to their remains; but their souls went up to the judgment seat unthought of, uncared for; no man, not even the minister who had vowed to watch for them, having said to them, Are you ready?— or warned them to flee from the wrath to come.

Is not this description too true of many a district and many a minister? We do not speak in anger; we do not speak in scorn: we ask the question solemnly and earnestly. It needs an answer. If ever there was a time when there should be "great searching of heart" and frank acknowledgment of unfaithfulness, it is now when God is visiting us—visiting us both in judgment and in mercy. We speak in brotherly kindness; surely the answer should not be of wrath and bitterness. And if this description be true, what sin must there be in ministers and people! How great must be the spiritual desolation that prevails! Surely there is something in such a case grievously wrong; something which calls for solemn self-examination in every minister; something which requires deep repentance.

The Tragedy of a Barren Ministry

Fields plowed and sown, yet yielding no fruit! Machinery constantly in motion, yet all without one particle of produce! Nets cast into the sea, and spread wide, yet no fishes enclosed! All this for years—for a lifetime! How strange! Yet it is true. There is neither fancy nor exaggeration in the matter. Question some ministers, and what other account can they give? They can tell you of sermons *preached*, but of sermons *blessed* they can say nothing. They can speak of discourses that were admired and praised, but of discourses that have been made effectual by the Holy Spirit they cannot speak. They can tell you how many have been baptized, how many communicants admitted; but of souls awakened, converted, ripening in grace, they can give no account. They can enumerate the sacraments they have dispensed; but as to whether any of them have been "times of refreshing" or times of awakening, they cannot say. They can tell you what and how many cases of discipline have passed through their hands; but whether any of these have issued in godly sorrow for sin, whether the professed penitents who were absolved by them gave evidence of being "washed and sanctified and justified," they can give no information; they never thought of such an issue!

They can tell what is the attendance at Sunday school, and what are the abilities of the teacher; but how many of these precious little ones whom they have vowed to feed are seeking the Lord they know not; or whether their teacher be a man of prayer and piety they cannot say. They can tell you the population of their parish, the number of their congregation, or the temporal condition of their flocks; but as to their spiritual state, how many have been awakened from the sleep of death, how many are followers of God as dear children, they cannot pretend to say. Perhaps they would deem it rashness and presumption, if not fanaticism, to inquire. And yet they have sworn, before men and angels, to *watch for their souls* as they that must give account! But oh, of what use are sermons, sacraments, schools, if *souls* are left to perish; if living religion be lost sight of; if the Holy Spirit be not sought; if men are left to grow up and die unpitied, unprayed for, unwarned!

For God's Glory and Man's Good

It was not so in other days. Our fathers really watched and preached for souls. They asked and they expected a blessing. Nor were they denied it. They were blessed in turning many to righteousness. Their lives record their successful labors. How refreshing the lives of those who lived only for the glory of God and the good of souls. There is something in their history that compels us to feel that they were ministers of Christ— true watchmen.

How cheering to read of Baxter and his labors at

Kidderminster! How solemn to hear of Venn and his preaching, in regard to which it is said that men "fell before him like slaked lime"! And in the much-blest labors of that man of God, the apostolic Whitefield, is there not much to humble us, as well as to stimulate? Of Tanner, who was himself awakened under Whitefield, we read that he "seldom preached one sermon in vain." Of Berridge and Hicks we are told that in their missionary tours throughout England they were blessed in one year to awaken four thousand souls. Oh, for these days again! Oh, for one day of Whitefield again!

Thus one has written: "The language we have been accustomed to adopt is this; we must use the means, and leave the event to God; we can do no more than employ the means; this is our duty and having done this we must leave the rest to Him who is the disposer of all things." Such language sounds well, for it seems to be an acknowledgment of our own nothingness, and to savor of submission to God's sovereignty; but it is only sound— it has not really any substance in it, for though there is truth stamped on *the face* of it, there is falsehood at *the root* of it. To talk of submission to God's sovereignty is one thing, but really to submit to it is another and quite different thing.

Submission Involves Renunciation

"Really to submit to God's sovereign disposal does always necessarily involve the deep renunciation of our own will in the matter concerned, and such a renunciation of the will can never be effected without a soul being brought through very severe and trying exercises of an inward and most humbling nature. Therefore, whilst we are quietly satisfied in using the means without obtaining the end, and this costs us no such painful inward exercise and deep humbling as that alluded to, if we think that we are leaving the affair to God's disposal, we deceive ourselves, and the truth in this matter is not in us.

"No; really to give anything to God implies that *the will*, which is emphatically *the heart*, has been *set on that thing*; and if *the heart* has indeed been *set* on the salvation of sinners as the end to be answered by the means we use, we can not possibly give up that end without, as was before observed, the heart being severely exercised and deeply pained by the renunciation of the will involved in it. When, therefore, we can be quietly content to use the means for saving souls without seeing them saved thereby, it is because there is no renunciation of the will—that is, no real giving up to God in the affair. The fact is, the will—that is, *the heart*—had never really been set upon this end; if it had, it could not possibly give up such an end without being *broken* by the sacrifice.

"When we can thus be satisfied to use the means without obtaining the end, and speak of it as though we were submitting to the Lord's disposal, we use a truth to hide a falsehood, exactly in the same way that those formalists in religion do, who continue in forms and duties without going beyond them, though they know they will not save them, and who, when they are warned of their danger and earnestly entreated to seek the Lord

with all the heart, reply by telling us they know they must repent and believe but that they cannot do either the one or the other of themselves and that they must wait till God gives them grace to do so. Now, this is a truth, absolutely considered; yet most of us can see that they are using it as a falsehood to cover and excuse a great insincerity of heart. We can readily perceive that if their hearts were really set upon salvation, they could not rest satisfied without it. Their contentedness is the result, not of heart-submission to God, but in reality of *heart indifference to the salvation of their own souls*.

Covering Falsehood With Truth

"Exactly so it is with us as ministers: when we can rest satisfied with using the means for saving souls without seeing them really saved, or we ourselves being broken-hearted by it, and at the same time quietly talk of leaving the event to God's disposal, we make use of a truth to cover and excuse a falsehood; for our ability to leave the matter thus is not, as we imagine, the result of heart-submission to God, but of heart-indifference to the salvation of the souls we deal with. No, truly, if the heart is really set on such an end, it must gain that end or break in losing it."

He that saved our souls has taught us to weep over the unsaved. Lord, let that mind be in us that was in Thee! Give us thy tears to weep; for, Lord, our hearts are hard toward our fellows. We can see thousands perish around us, and our sleep never be disturbed; no vision of

23

their awful doom ever scaring us, no cry from their lost souls ever turning our peace into bitterness.

Our families, our schools, our congregations, not to speak of our cities at large, our land, our world, might well send us daily to our knees; for the loss of even *one soul* is terrible beyond conception. Eye has not seen, nor ear heard, nor has entered the heart of man, what a soul in hell must suffer forever. Lord, give us bowels of mercies! "What a mystery! The soul and eternity of one man depends upon the voice of another!"

IV

MINISTERIAL CONFESSION

"Remember therefore from whence thou art fallen, and repent, and do the first works; or else I will come unto thee quickly, and will remove thy candlestick out of his place, except thou repent."—REVELATION 2:5.

IN THE YEAR 1651 the Church of Scotland, feeling in regard to her ministers "how deep their hand was in the transgression, and that ministers had no small accession to the drawing on of the judgments that were upon the land," drew up what they called a humble acknowledgment of the sins of the ministry. This document is a striking and searching one. It is perhaps one of the fullest, most faithful and most impartial confessions of ministerial sin ever made. A few extracts from it will suitably introduce this chapter on ministerial confession. It begins with confessing

25

sins before entrance on the ministry:

"Lightness and profanity in conversation, unsuitable to that holy calling which they did intend, not thoroughly repented of. Not studying to be in Christ before they be in the ministry; nor to have the practical knowledge and experience of the mystery of the gospel in themselves before they preach it to others. Neglecting to fit themselves for the work of the ministry, in not improving prayer and fellowship with God, opportunities of a lively ministry, and other means, and not mourning for these neglects. Not studying self-denial, nor resolving to take up the cross of Christ. Negligence to entertain a sight and sense of sin and misery; not wrestling against corruption, nor studying mortification and subduedness of spirit."

Of entrance on the ministry it thus speaks:

"Entering to the ministry without respect to a commission from Jesus Christ, by which it hath come to pass that many have run unsent. Entering to the ministry not from the love of Christ, nor from a desire to honor God in gaining of souls, but for a name and for a livelihood in the world notwithstanding a solemn declaration to the contrary at admission."

Of the sins after entrance on the ministry, it thus searchingly enumerates:

"Ignorance of God, want of nearness with Him, and taking up little of God in reading, meditating and speaking of Him. Exceeding great selfishness in all that we do; acting from ourselves, for ourselves and to ourselves. Not caring how unfaithful and negligent others were, so being it might contribute a testimony to our faithfulness

26

and diligence, but being rather content, if not rejoicing, at their faults. Least delight in those things wherein lieth our nearest communion with God; great inconstancy in our walk with God, and neglect of acknowledging Him in all our ways. In going about duties, least careful of those things which are most remote from the eyes of men. Seldom in secret prayer with God, except to fit for public performance; and even that much neglected, or gone about very superficially.

Glad to Find Excuses

"Glad to find excuses for the neglect of duties. Neglecting the reading of Scriptures in secret, for edifying ourselves as Christians; only reading them in so far as may fit us for our duty as ministers, and ofttimes neglecting that. Not given to reflect upon our own ways, nor allowing conviction to have a thorough work upon us; deceiving ourselves by resting upon absence from and abhorrence of evils from the light of a natural conscience, and looking upon the same as an evidence of a real change of state and nature. Evil guarding of and watching over the heart, and carelessness in self-searching; which makes much unacquaintedness with ourselves and estrangedness from God. Not guarding nor wrestling against seen and known evils, especially our predominants. A facility to be drawn away with the temptations of the time, and other particular temptations, according to our inclinations and fellowship.

"Instability and wavering in the ways of God,

through the fears of persecutions, hazard, or loss of esteem; and declining duties because of the fear of jealousies and reproaches. Not esteeming the cross of Christ and sufferings for His name, honorable, but rather shifting sufferings from self-love. Deadness of spirit, after all the sore strokes of God upon the land. Little conscience made of secret humiliation and fasting, by ourselves apart and in our families, that we might mourn for our own and the land's guiltiness and great backslidings; and little applying of public humiliation to our own hearts. Finding of our own pleasure, when the Lord calls for our humiliation.

"Not laying to heart the sad and heavy sufferings of the people of God abroad, and the not-thriving of the kingdom of Jesus Christ and the power of godliness among them. Refined hypocrisy; desiring to appear what, indeed, we are not. Studying more to learn the language of God's people than their exercise. Artificial confessing of sin, without repentance; professing to declare iniquity, and not resolving to be sorry for sin. Confession in secret much slighted, even of those things whereof we are convicted. No reformation, after solemn acknowledgments and private vows; thinking ourselves exonerated after confession. Readier to search out and censure faults in others than to see or deal with them in ourselves. Accounting of our estate and way according to the estimation that others have of us. Estimation of men, as they agree with or disagree from us.

"Not fearing to meet with trials, but presuming, in our own strength, to go through them unshaken. Not learning to fear, by the falls of gracious men, nor mourn-

ing and praying for them. Not observing particular deliv-
erances and punishments, not improving of them, for the
honor of God, and the edification of ourselves and others. Little or no mourning for the corruption of our
nature, and less groaning under, and longing to be delivered from, that body of death, the bitter root of all our
other evils.

"Fruitless conversing ordinarily with others, for the
worse rather than for the better. Foolish jesting away of
time with impertinent and useless discourse, very unbe-
coming the ministers of the gospel. Spiritual purposes
often dying in our hands when they are begun by others.
Carnal familiarity with natural, wicked and malignant
men, whereby they are hardened, the people of God
stumbled, and we ourselves blunted.

Loving Pleasure More Than God

"Slighting of fellowship with those by whom we
might profit. Desiring more to converse with those that
might better us by their talents than with such as might
edify us by their graces. Not studying opportunities of
doing good to others. Shifting of prayer and other duties
when called thereto—choosing rather to omit the same
than that we should be put to them ourselves. Abusing
of time in frequent recreation and pastimes and loving
our pleasures more than God. Taking little or no time to
Christian discourse with young men trained up for the
ministry. Common and ordinary discourse on the Lord's
Day. Slighting Christian admonition from any of our

flocks or others, as being below us; and ashamed to take light and warning from private Christians. Dislike of, or bitterness against, such as deal freely with us by admonition or reproof, and not dealing faithfully with others who would welcome it off our hands.

"Not praying for men of a contrary judgment, but using reservedness and distance from them; being more ready to speak *of* them than to them or to God *for* them. Not weighed with the failings and miscarriages of others, but rather taking advantage thereof for justifying ourselves. Talking of and sporting at the faults of others, rather than compassionating of them. No due painstaking in religious ordering of our families, nor studying to be patterns to other families in the government of ours. Hasty anger and passion in our families and conversation with others. Covetousness, worldly-mindedness, and an inordinate desire after the things of this life, upon which followeth a neglect of the duties of our calling, and our being taken up for the most part with the things of the world. Want of hospitality and charity to the members of Christ. Not cherishing godliness in the people; and some being afraid of it and hating the people of God for piety, and studying to bear down and quench the work of the Spirit amongst them.

Trusting in Our Own Ability

"Not entertaining that edge of spirit in ministerial duties which we found at the first entry to the ministry. Great neglect of reading, and other preparation; or preparation merely literal and bookish, making an idol of a book, which hindereth communion with God; or presuming on bygone assistance, and praying little. Trusting to gifts, talents, and pains taken for preparation, whereby God is provoked to blast good matter, well ordered and worded. Careless in employing Christ, and drawing virtue out of Him, for enabling us to preach in the Spirit and in power. In praying for assistance we pray more for assistance to the messenger than to the message which we carry, not caring what becomes of the Word, if we be with some measure of assistance carried on in the duty. The matter we bring forth is not seriously recommended to God by prayer, to be quickened to His people. Neglect of prayer after the Word is preached.

"Neglect to warn, in preaching, of snares and sins in public affairs by some; and too much, too frequent, and unnecessary speaking by others of public business and transactions. Exceeding great neglect and unskillfulness to set forth the excellences and usefulness of (and the necessity of an interest in) Jesus Christ, and the new covenant, which ought to be the great subject of a minister's study and preaching. Speaking of Christ more by hearsay than from knowledge and experience, or any real impression of Him upon the heart. The way of most ministers' preaching too legal. Want of sobriety in preaching the gospel; not savoring anything but what is new; so that the substantials of religion bear but little bulk.

"Not preaching Christ in the simplicity of the gospel, nor ourselves the people's servants, for Christ's sake. Preaching of Christ, not that the people may know Him, but that they may think we know much of Him. Preach-

ing about Christ's leaving of the world without broken-
ness of heart, or stirring up of ourselves to take hold of
Him. Not preaching with bowels of compassion to them
that are in hazard to perish. Preaching against public
sins, neither in such a way, nor for such an end, as we
ought—for the gaining of souls and drawing men out of
their sins; but rather because it is to our advantage to say
something of these evils.

Attitude Toward Our Opponents

"Bitterness, instead of zeal, in speaking against
malignants, sectarians and other scandalous persons; and
unfaithfulness therein. Not studying to know the particular condition of the souls of the people, that we may
speak to them accordingly; nor keeping a particular record
thereof, though convinced of the usefulness of this. Not
carefully choosing what may be most profitable and edifying, and want of wisdom in application to the several
conditions of souls, not so careful to bring home the
point by application as to find out the doctrine, nor
speaking the same with that reverence which becomes
His word and message.

"Choosing texts whereon we have something to
say, rather than those suited to the conditions of souls
and times, and frequent preaching of the same things,
that we may not be put to the pains of new study. Such
a way of reading, preaching and prayer as puts us in these
duties further from God. Too soon satisfied in the discharge of duties, and holding off challenges of conscience

with excuses. Indulging the body and wasting much time idly. Too much eyeing our own credit and applause; and being pleased with it when we get it, and unsatisfied when it is wanting. Timorousness in delivering God's message, letting people die in reigning sins without warning. Studying the discharge of duties rather to free ourselves from censure than to approve ourselves to God.

"Not making all the counsel of God known to His people; and particularly, not giving testimony in times of defection. Not studying to profit by our own doctrine, nor the doctrine of others. For most part preaching as if we ourselves were not concerned in the message which we carry to the people. Not rejoicing at the conversion of sinners, but content with the unthriving of the Lord's work amongst His people as suiting best with our minds; fearing, if they should thrive better we should be more put to it, and less esteemed of by them—many, in preaching and practice, bearing down the power of godliness. We preach not as before God, but as to men; as doth appear by the different pains in our preparation to speak to our ordinary hearers and to others to whom we would approve ourselves.

"Negligent, lazy, and partial visiting of the sick. If they be poor we go once, and only when sent for; if they be rich and of better note, we go oftener and unsent for. Not knowing how to speak with the tongue of the learned a word in season to the weary.

"Lazy and negligent in catechising. Not preparing our hearts before, nor wrestling with God for a blessing to it, because of the ordinariness and apprehended easiness of it, whereby the Lord's name is much taken in vain, and the people little profited. Looking on that exercise as a work below us, and not condescending to study a right and profitable way of instructing the Lord's people. Partial in catechising, passing by those that are rich and of better quality, though many of such stand ordinarily in great need of instruction. Not waiting upon and following the ignorant but often passionately upbraiding them."

These are solemn confessions—the confessions of men who knew the nature of that ministry on which they had entered, and who were desirous of approving themselves to Him who had called them, that they might give in their account with joy and not with grief.

Confessing Our Shortcomings

Let us, as they did, deal honestly with ourselves. Our confessions ought to be no less ample and searching.

1. *We have been unfaithful.* The fear of man and the love of his applause have often made us afraid. We have been unfaithful to our own souls, to our flocks, and to our brethren; unfaithful in the pulpit, in visiting, in discipline, in the church. In the discharge of every one of the duties of our stewardship there has been grievous unfaithfulness. Instead of the special particularization of the sin reproved, there has been the vague allusion. Instead of the bold reproof, there has been the timid hint. Instead of the uncompromising condemnation, there has been the feeble disapproval. Instead of the unswerving

consistency of a holy life whose uniform tenor should be a protest against the world and a rebuke of sin, there has been such an amount of unfaithfulness in our walk and conversation, in our daily deportment and intercourses with others, that any degree of faithfulness we have been enabled to manifest on the Lord's Day is almost neutralized by the want of circumspection which our weekday life exhibits.

Archbishop Ussher's Example

Few men ever lived a life so busy and so devoted to God as Ussher, Archbishop of Armagh. His learning, habits of business, station, friends, all contributed to keep his hands every moment full; and then his was a soul that seemed continually to hear a voice saying: "Redeem the time, for the days are evil." Early, too, did he begin, for at ten years of age he was hopefully converted by a sermon preached on Romans 12:1: *"I beseech you therefore, brethren, by the mercies of God, that ye present your bodies a living sacrifice."* He was a painstaking, laborious preacher of the Word for fifty-five years.

Yet hear him on his death-bed! How he clings to Christ's righteousness alone, and sees in himself, even after such a life, only sin and want. The last words he was heard to utter were about one o'clock in the afternoon, and these words were uttered in a loud voice: *"But, Lord, in special forgive me my sins of omission."* It was *omissions*, says his biographer, he begged forgiveness of with his most fervent last breath—he

35

who was never known to omit an hour, but who employed the shred ends of his life for his great Lord and Master! The very day he took his last sickness, he rose up from writing one of his great works and went out to visit a sick woman, to whom he spoke so fitly and fully that you would have taken him to have spoken of heaven before he came there. Yet this man was oppressed with a sense of his *omissions!*

Reader, what think you of yourself—your undone duties, your unimproved hours, times of prayer omitted, your shrinking from unpleasant work and putting it on others, your being content to sit under your vine and fig tree without using all efforts for the souls of others? *"Lord, in special forgive me my sins of omission!"*

Hear the confession of Edwards, in regard both to personal and ministerial sins: "Often I have had very affecting views of my own sinfulness and vileness; very frequently to such a degree as to hold me in a kind of loud weeping, sometimes for a considerable time together, so that I have often been forced to shut myself up. I have had a vastly greater sense of my own wickedness, and the badness of my heart, than ever I had before my conversion. My wickedness, as I am in myself, has long appeared to me perfectly ineffable, swallowing up all thought and imagination. I know not how to express better what my sins appear to me to be than by heaping infinite upon infinite, and multiplying infinite by infinite. When I look into my heart and take a view of my wickedness, it looks like an abyss infinitely deeper than hell. And yet it seems to me that my conviction of sin is exceedingly small and faint: it is enough to amaze me that I have no more sense of my sin. I have greatly longed of late for a broken heart, and to lie low before God."

Worldliness Stunts the Conscience

2. *We have been carnal and unspiritual.* * The tone of our life has been low and earthly. Associating too much and too intimately with the world, we have in a great measure become accustomed to its ways. Hence our tastes have been vitiated, our consciences blunted, and that sensitive tenderness of feeling which, while it turns not back from suffering yet shrinks from the remotest contact with sin, has worn off and given place to an amount of callousness of which we once, in fresher days, believed ourselves incapable.

Perhaps we can call to mind a time when our views and aims were fixed upon a standard of almost unearthly elevation, and, contrasting these with our present state, we are startled at the painful changes. And besides intimacy with the world, other causes have operated in producing this deterioration in the spirituality of our minds. The study of truth in its dogmatical more than in its devotional form has robbed it of its freshness and power; daily, hourly occupation

---

* "Our want of usefulness is much oftener to be ascribed to our want of spirituality than to any want of natural ability."—*Fuller.* "I see that spirituality of mind is the main qualification for the work of the ministry."—*Urquhart.*

in the routine of ministerial labor has engendered
formality and coldness; continual employment in the
most solemn duties of our office, such as dealing with
souls in private about their immortal welfare, or guiding the meditations and devotions of God's assembled
people, or handling the sacramental symbols—this,
gone about often with so little prayer and mixed with
so little faith, has tended grievously to divest us of
that profound reverence and godly fear which ever
ought to possess and pervade us. How truly, and with
what emphasis, we may say: *"I am carnal, sold under
sin"* (Romans 7:14). The world has not been crucified
to us, nor we unto the world; the flesh, with its members, has not been mortified. What a sad effect all this
has had, not only upon our peace of soul, on our
growth in grace, but upon the success of our ministry!

3. *We have been selfish.* We have shrunk from toil,
difficulty and endurance, counting not only our lives
dear unto us, but even our temporal ease and comfort.
We have sought to please ourselves, instead of obeying
Romans 15:2: *"Let every one of us please his neighbor for his
good to edification."* We have not borne *"one another's
burdens, and so fulfill the law of Christ"* (Galatians 6:2).
We have been worldly and covetous. We have not pre-
sented ourselves unto God as "living sacrifices, laying
ourselves, our lives, our substance, our time, our strength,
our faculties—our all—upon His alter. We seem alto-
gether to have lost sight of this self-sacrificing principle
on which even as Christians, but much more as ministers, we are called upon to act. We have had little idea

of anything like *sacrifice* at all. Up to the point where a sacrifice was demanded, we may have been willing to go, but there we stood; counting it unnecessary, perhaps calling it imprudent and unadvised, to proceed further. Yet ought not the life of every Christian, especially of every minister, to be a life of self-sacrifice and self-denial throughout, even as was the life of Him who "pleased not himself"?

4. *We have been slothful.* We have been sparing of our toil. We have not endured hardness as good soldiers of Jesus Christ. Even when we have been instant in season, we have not been so out of season; neither have we sought to gather up the fragments of our time, that not a moment might be thrown idly or unprofitably away. Precious hours and days have been wasted in sloth, in company, in pleasure, in idle or desultory reading, that might have been devoted to the closet, the study, the pulpit or the meeting! Indolence, self-indulgence, fickleness, flesh-pleasing, have eaten like a canker into our ministry, arresting the blessing and marring our success.

It cannot be said of us, *"For my name's sake [thou] hast labored, and hast not fainted"* (Revelation 2:3). Alas! we have fainted, or at least grown "weary in well-doing." We have not made conscience of our work. We have not dealt honestly with the church to which we pledged the vows of ordination. We have dealt deceitfully with God, whose servants we profess to be. We have manifested but little of the unwearied, self-denying love with which, as shepherds, we ought to have watched over the flocks

39

committed to our care. We have fed ourselves, and not the flock.*

5. *We have been cold.* Even when diligent, how little warmth and glow! The whole soul is not poured into the duty, and hence it wears too often the repulsive air of routine and form. We do not speak and act like men in earnest. Our words are feeble, even when sound and true; our looks are careless, even when our words are weighty; and our tones betray the apathy which both words and looks disguise. Love is wanting, deep love, love strong as death, love such as made Jeremiah weep in secret places for the pride of Israel, and Paul speak "even weeping" of the enemies of the cross of Christ. In preaching and visiting, in counseling and reproving, what formality, what coldness, how little tenderness and affection! "Oh that I was all heart," said Rowland Hill, "and soul, and spirit, to tell

---

* Hear Richard Baxter's statement of his usual ministerial duties, in answer to some enemies who taunted him with idleness. "The worst I wish you is that you had my ease instead of your labor. I have reason to take myself for the least of all saints, and yet I fear not to tell the accuser that I take labor of most tradesmen in the town to be a pleasure to the body in comparison with mine, though I would not exchange it with the greatest prince. Their labor preserveth health and mine consumeth it; they work in ease, and I in continual pain; they have hours and days of recreation, I have scarce time to eat and drink. Nobody molesteth them for their labor, but the more I do, the more hatred and trouble I draw upon me." This is "spending and being spent"; this is an example worthy of imitation.

the glorious gospel of Christ to perishing multitudes!"

Afraid to Tell the Whole Truth

6. *We have been timid*. Fear has often led us to smooth down or generalize truths which if broadly stated must have brought hatred and reproach upon us. We have thus often failed to declare to our people the whole counsel of God. We have shrunk from reproving, rebuking and exhorting with all longsuffering and doctrine. We have feared to alienate friends, or to awaken the wrath of enemies. Hence our preaching of the law has been feeble and straitened; and hence our preaching of a free gospel has been yet more vague, uncertain and timorous. We are greatly deficient in that majestic boldness and nobility of spirit which peculiarly marked Luther, Calvin, Knox, and the mighty men of the Reformation. Of Luther it was said, "Every word was a thunderbolt."

7. *We have been wanting in solemnity*. In reading the lives of Howe or Baxter, of Brainerd or Edwards, we are in company with men who in solemnity of deportment and gravity of demeanor were truly of the apostolic school. We feel that these men must have carried weight with them, in both their words and their lives. We see also the contrast between ourselves and them in respect of that deep solemnity of air and tone which made men feel that they walked with God. How deeply ought we to be abased at our levity, frivolity, flippancy, vain mirth, foolish talking and jesting, by which grievous injury has been

41

done to souls, the progress of the saints retarded, and the world countenanced in its wretched vanities.

Preaching Self Instead of Christ

8. *We have preached ourselves, not Christ.* We have sought applause, courted honor, been avaricious of fame and jealous of our reputation. We have preached too often so as to exalt ourselves instead of magnifying Christ, so as to draw men's eyes to ourselves instead of fixing them on Him and His cross. Nay, and have we not often preached Christ for the very purpose of getting honor to ourselves? Christ, in the sufferings of His first coming and the glory of His second, has not been the Alpha and Omega, the first and the last, of all our sermons.

9. *We have used words of man's wisdom.* We have forgotten Paul's resolution to avoid the enticing words of man's wisdom, lest he should make the cross of Christ of none effect. We have reversed his reasoning as well as his resolution, and acted as if by well-studied, well-polished, well-reasoned discourses, we could so gild and beautify the cross as to make it no longer repulsive, but irresistibly attractive to the carnal eye! Hence we have often sent men home well satisfied with themselves, convinced that they were religious because they were affected by our eloquence, touched by our appeals or persuaded by our arguments. In this way we have made the cross of Christ of none effect and sent souls to hell with a lie in their right hand. Thus by avoiding the offense of the

cross and the foolishness of preaching we have had to labor in vain, and mourn over an unblest, unfruitful ministry.

10. *We have not fully preached a free gospel.* We have been afraid of making it *too free*, lest men should be led into licentiousness; as if it were possible to preach too free a gospel, or as if its *freeness* could lead men into sin. It is only a free gospel that can bring peace, and it is only a free gospel that can make men holy. Luther's preaching was summed up in these two points—"that we are justified by faith alone, and that we must be assured that we are justified"; and it was this that he urged his brother Brentius to preach; and it was by such free, full, bold preaching of the glorious gospel, untrammeled by works, merits, terms, conditions, and unclouded by the fancied humility of doubts, fears, uncertainties, that such blessed success accompanied his labors. Let us go and do likewise. Allied to this is the necessity of insisting on the sinner's *immediate* turning to God, and demanding in the Master's name the sinner's *immediate* surrender of heart to Christ. Strange that sudden conversions should be so much disliked by some ministers. They are the most scriptural of all conversions.

Too Little Emphasis on God's Word

11. *We have not duly studied and honored the Word of God.* We have given a greater prominence to man's writings, man's opinions, man's systems in our studies

than to the Word. We have drunk more out of human cisterns than divine. We have held more communion with man than with God. Hence the mold and fashion of our spirits, our lives, our words, have been derived more from man than from God. We must study the Bible more. We must steep our souls in it. We must not only lay it up within us, but transfuse it through the whole texture of the soul.

12. *We have not been men of prayer*. The spirit of prayer has slumbered amongst us. The closet has been too little frequented and delighted in. We have allowed business, study or active labor to interfere with our closet-hours. And the feverish atmosphere in which both the church and nation are enveloped has found its way into our closet, disturbing the sweet calm of its blessed solitude. Sleep, company, idle visiting, foolish talking and jesting, idle reading, unprofitable occupations, engross time that might have been redeemed for prayer.

Time for Everything but Prayer

Why is there so little anxiety to get time to pray? Why is there so little forethought in the laying out of time and employments so as to secure a large portion of each day for prayer? Why is there so much speaking, yet so little prayer? Why is there so much running to and fro, yet so little prayer? Why so much bustle and business, yet so little prayer? Why so many meetings with our fellowmen, yet so few meetings with God? Why so little being alone, so little thirsting of the soul for the calm, sweet hours of unbroken solitude, when God and His child hold fellowship together as if they could never part? It is the want of these solitary hours that not only injures our own growth in grace but makes us such unprofitable members of the church of Christ, and that renders our lives useless. In order to grow in grace, we must be much *alone*. It is not in society—even Christian society—that the soul grows most rapidly and vigorously. In *one single* quiet hour of prayer it will often make more progress than in days of company with others. It is in the desert that the dew falls freshest and the air is purest. So with the soul. It is when none but God is nigh; when His presence alone, like the desert air in which there is mingled no noxious breath of man, surrounds and pervades the soul; it is then that the eye gets the clearest, simplest view of eternal certainties; it is then that the soul gathers in wondrous refreshment and power and energy.

And so it is also in this way that we become truly useful to others. It is when coming out fresh from communion with God that we go forth to do His work successfully. It is in the closet that we get our vessels so filled with blessing, that, when we come forth, we cannot contain it to ourselves but must, as by a blessed necessity, pour it out whithersoever we go. We cannot say, as did Isaiah: "*My Lord, I stand continually upon the watchtower in the daytime, and I am let in my ward whole nights*" (Isaiah 21:8). Our life has not been a lying-in-wait for the voice of God. "*Speak, Lord; for thy servant heareth*" (1 Samuel 3:9) has not been the attitude of our

45

souls, the guiding principle of our lives. Nearness to God, fellowship with God, waiting upon God, resting in God, have been too little the characteristic either of our private or of our ministerial walk. Hence our example has been so powerless, our labors so unsuccessful, our sermons so meager, our whole ministry so fruitless and feeble.

Seeking the Spirit's Strength

13. *We have not honored the Spirit of God.* It may be that in words we have recognized His agency, but we have not kept this continually before our eyes, and the eyes of the people. We have not given Him the glory that is due unto His name. We have not sought His teaching, His anointing—the *"unction from the Holy One, [whereby] ye know all things"* (1 John 2:20). Neither in the study of the Word nor in the preaching of it to others have we duly acknowledged His office as the Enlightener of the understanding, the Revealer of the truth, the Testifier and Glorifier of Christ. We have grieved Him by the dishonor done to His person as the third person of the glorious Trinity; and we have grieved Him by the slight put upon His office as the Teacher, the Convincer, the Comforter, the Sanctifier. Hence He has almost departed from us, and left us to reap the fruit of our own perversity and unbelief. Besides, we have grieved Him by our inconsistent walk, by our want of circumspection, by our worldly-mindedness, by our unholiness, by our prayerlessness, by our unfaithfulness, by our want of so-

lemnity, by a life and conversation so little in conformity with the character of a disciple or the office of ambassador.

An old Scottish minister thus writes concerning himself: "I find a want of the Spirit—of the power and demonstration of the Spirit—in praying, speaking, and exhorting; that whereby men are mainly convinced, and whereby they are a terror and a wonder unto others, so as they stand in awe of them; that glory and majesty whereby respect and reverence are procured; that whereby Christ's sermons were differenced from those of the Scribes and Pharisees; which I judge to be the beams of God's majesty and of the Spirit of holiness breaking out and shining through His people. But my foul garments are on! Woe is me! The crown of glory and majesty is fallen off my head; my words are weak and carnal, not mighty; whereby contempt is bred. No remedy for this but humility, self-loathing and a striving to maintain fellowship with God."

Too Little Imitation of Christ

14. *We have had little of the mind of Christ.* We have come far short of the example of the apostles, much more of Christ; we are far behind the servants, much farther behind the Master. We have had little of the grace, the compassion, the meekness, the lowliness, the love of God's eternal Son. His weeping over Jerusalem is a feeling in which we have but little heartfelt sympathy. His "seeking of the lost" is little imitated by us. His unwea-

ried "teaching of the multitudes" we shrink from as too much for flesh and blood. His days of fasting, His nights of watchfulness and prayer, are not fully realized as models for us to copy. His counting not His life dear unto Him that He might glorify the Father and finish the work given Him to do, is but little remembered by us as the principle on which we are to act. Yet surely we are to follow His steps; the servant is to walk where his Master has led the way; the under shepherd is to be what the Chief Shepherd was. We must not seek rest or ease in a world where He whom we love had none.

V

REVIVAL IN THE MINISTRY

IT IS EASIER to speak or write about revival than to set about it. There is so much rubbish to be swept out, so many self-raised hindrances to be dealt with, so many old habits to be overcome, so much sloth and easy-mindedness to be contended with, so much of ministerial routine to be broken through, and so much crucifixion, both of self and of the world, to be undergone. As Christ said of the unclean spirit which the disciples could not cast out, so we may say of these: "This kind goeth not out but by prayer and fasting."

So thought a minister in the seventeenth century; for, after lamenting the evils both of his life and his ministry, he thus resolves to set about their renewal:

"(1) In imitation of Christ and His apostles, and to get good done, I purpose to rise timely every morning.

"(2) To prepare as soon as I am up some work to be

49

done, and how and when to do it; to engage my heart to it; and at even to call myself to account and to mourn over my failings.

"(3) To spend a sufficient portion of time every day in prayer, reading, meditating, spiritual exercises: morning, midday, evening, and ere I go to bed.

"(4) Once in the month, either the end or middle of it, I keep a day of humiliation for the public condition, for the Lord's people and their sad condition, for raising up the work and people of God.

"(5) I spend, besides this, one day for my own private condition, in fighting against spiritual evils and to get my heart more holy, or to get some special exercise accomplished, once in six months.

"(6) I spend once every week four hours over and above my daily portion in private, for some special causes relating either to myself or others.

"(7) To spend some time on Saturday, towards night, for preparation for the Lord's Day.

"(8) To spend six or seven days together, once a year, when most convenient, wholly and only on spiritual accounts."

Today's Need for Revival

Such was the way in which he set about personal and ministerial revival. Let us take an example from him. If he needed it much, we need it more.

In the fifth and sixth centuries, Gildas and Salvian arose to alarm and arouse a careless church and a formal ministry. In the sixteenth, such was the task which de-volved on the Reformers. In the seventeenth, Baxter, among others, took a prominent part in stimulating the languid piety and dormant energies of his fellow minis-ters. In the eighteenth, God raised up some choice and noble men to awaken the church and lead the way to a higher and bolder career of ministerial duty. The present century stands no less in need of some such stimulating influence. We have experienced many symptoms of life, but still the mass is not quickened. We require some new Baxter to arouse us by his voice and his example. It is melancholy to see the amount of ministerial languor and inefficiency that still overspreads our land. How long, O Lord, how long!

The infusion of new life into the ministry ought to be the object of more direct and special effort, as well as of more united and fervent prayer. The prayers of Christians ought to be more largely directed to the students, the preachers, the ministers of the Christian church. It is a *living* ministry that our country needs; and without such a ministry it can not long expect to escape the judgments of God. *We need men that will spend and be spent—that will labor and pray—that will watch and weep for souls.*

How Myconius Learned His Lesson

In the life of Myconius, the friend of Luther, as given by Melchior Adam, we have the following beauti-ful and striking account of an event which proved the turning point in his history and led him to devote his

51

energies to the cause of Christ. The first night that he entered the monastery, intending to become a monk, he dreamed; and it seemed as if he was ranging a vast wilderness alone. Suddenly a guide appeared and led him onwards to a most lovely vale, watered by a pleasant stream of which he was not permitted to taste, and then to a marble fountain of pure water. He tried to kneel and drink, when, lo! a crucified Savior stood forth to view, from whose wounds gushed the copious stream. In a moment his guide flung him into the fountain. His mouth met the flowing wounds and he drank most sweetly, never to thirst again!

No sooner was he refreshed himself than he was led away by his guide to be taught what great things he was yet to do for the crucified One whose precious wounds had poured the living water into his soul. He came to a wide stretching plain covered with waving grain. His guide ordered him to reap. He excused himself by saying that he was wholly unskilled in such labor. "What you know not you shall learn," was the reply. They came nearer, and he saw a solitary reaper toiling at the sickle with such prodigious effort as if he were determined to reap the whole field himself. The guide ordered him to join this laborer, and seizing a sickle, showed him how to proceed.

Again, the guide led him to a hill. He surveyed the vast plain beneath him, and, wondering, asked how long it would take to reap such a field with so few laborers. "Before winter the last sickle must be thrust in," replied his guide. "Proceed with all your might. The Lord of the harvest will send more reapers soon." Wearied with his labor, Myconius rested for a little. Again the crucified One was at his side, wasted and marred in form. The guide laid his hand on Myconius, saying: "You must be conformed to Him."

With these words the dreamer awoke. But he awoke to a life of zeal and love. He found the Savior for his own soul, and he went forth to preach of Him to others. He took his place by the side of that noble reaper, Martin Luther. He was stimulated by his example and toiled with him in the vast field till laborers arose on every side and the harvest was reaped before the winter came. The lesson to us is, thrust in your sickles. The fields are white, and they are wide in compass; the laborers are few, but there are some devoted ones toiling there already. In other years we have seen Whitefield and Hill putting forth their enormous efforts, as if they would reap the whole field alone. Let us join ourselves to such men, and the Lord of the harvest will not leave us to toil alone.

Reaping the Great Harvest

"When do you intend to stop?" was the question once put by a friend to Rowland Hill. "Not till we have carried all before us," was the prompt reply. Such is our answer too. The fields are vast, the grain whitens, the harvest waves; and through grace we shall go forth with our sickles, never to rest till we shall lie down where the Lamb himself shall lead us, by the living fountains of waters, where God shall wipe off the sweat of toil from our weary foreheads and dry up all the tears of earth from our weeping eyes. Some of us are young and fresh; many days may yet be, in the providence of God, before us.

These must be days of strenuous, ceaseless, persevering, and, if God bless us, successful toil. We shall labor till we are worn out and laid to rest.

Vincent, the nonconformist minister, in his small volume on the great plague and fire in London, entitled "God's Terrible Voice in the City," gives a description of the manner in which the faithful ministers who remained amid the danger discharged their solemn duties to the dying inhabitants, and of the manner in which the terror-stricken multitudes hung with breathless eagerness upon their lips, to drink in salvation ere the dreaded pestilence had swept them away to the tomb. Churches were flung open, but the pulpits were silent, for there was none to occupy them; the hirelings had fled.

Preaching to Plague Victims

Then did God's faithful band of persecuted ones come forth from their hiding places to fill the forsaken pulpits. Then did they stand up in the midst of the dying and the dead, to proclaim eternal life to men who were expecting death before the morrow. They preached in season and out of season. Weekday or Sunday was the same to them. The hour might be canonical or uncanonical, it mattered not; they did not stand upon nice points of ecclesiastical regularity or irregularity; they lifted up their voices like trumpets, and spared not. Every sermon might be their last. Graves were lying open around them; life seemed now not merely a handbreadth but a hairbreadth; death was nearer now than ever; eternity stood out in all its vast reality; souls were felt to be precious; opportunities were no longer to be trifled away; every hour possessed a value beyond the wealth of kingdoms; the world was now a passing, vanishing shadow, and man's days on earth had been cut down from threescore years and ten into the twinkling of an eye!

Oh, how they preached! No polished periods, no learned arguments, no labored paragraphs, chilled their appeals or rendered their discourses unintelligible. No fear of man, no love of popular applause, no everscrupulous dread of strong expressions, no fear of *excitement* or enthusiasm, prevented them from pouring out the whole fervor of their hearts, that yearned with tenderness unutterable over dying souls.

"Old Time," says Vincent, "seemed to stand at the head of the pulpit with his great scythe, saying with a hoarse voice, 'Work while it is called to-day: at night I will mow thee down.' Grim Death seemed to stand at the side of the pulpit, with its sharp arrow, saying, 'Do thou shoot God's arrows, and I will shoot mine.' The grave seemed to lie open at the foot of the pulpit, with dust in her bosom, saying—

> 'Louden thy cry
>   To God,
>   To men
> And now fulfill thy *trust*;
> Here thou must lie—
>   Mouth stopped,
>   Breath gone
> And silent in the dust.'

55

"Ministers now had awakening calls to seriousness and fervor in their ministerial work, to preach on the side and brink of the pit into which thousands were tumbling. There was such a vast concourse of people in the churches where these ministers were to be found that they could not many times come near the pulpit doors for the press, but were forced to climb over the pews to them; and such a face was seen in the assemblies as seldom was seen before in London; such eager looks, such open ears, such greedy attention, as if every word would be eaten which dropped from the mouths of the ministers."

Should We Ever Be Less Earnest?

Thus did they preach and thus did they hear in those days of terror and death. Men were in earnest then, both in speaking and in hearing. There was no coldness, no languor, no studied oratory. Truly they preached as dying men to dying men. But the question is, *Should it ever be otherwise?* Should there ever be less fervor in preaching or less eagerness in hearing than there was then? True, life *was a little* shorter then, but that was all. Death and its issues are still the same. Eternity is still the same. The soul is still the same. Only one small element was thrown in then which does not always exist to such an extent; namely, the increased shortness of life. But that was all the difference.

Unbelief Weakens Our Testimony

Why then should our preaching be less fervent, our appeals less affectionate, our importunity less urgent? We are a few steps farther from the shore of eternity; that is all. Time may be a little stronger than it was then, yet only a very little. Its everlasting issues are still as momentous, as unchangeable. Surely it is *our unbelief* that makes the difference! It is unbelief that makes ministers so cold in their preaching, so slothful in visiting, and so remiss in all their sacred duties. It is unbelief that chills the life and straitens the heart. It is unbelief that makes ministers handle eternal realities with such irreverence. It is unbelief that makes them ascend with so light a step "that awful place the pulpit,"* to deal with immortal beings about heaven and hell.

Hear one of Richard Baxter's appeals: "I have been ready to wonder, when I have heard such weighty things delivered, how people can forbear crying out in the congregation; much more how they can rest till they have gone to their ministers and learned what they should do. Oh, that heaven and hell should work no more upon men! Oh that everlastingness should work no more! Oh, how can you forbear when you are alone to think what it is to be everlastingly in joy or in torment! I wonder that such thoughts do not break your sleep; and that they come not in your mind when you are about your labor! I wonder how you can almost do anything else; how you

---

* A late minister used to say that he always liked to go from his knees to that awful place—the pulpit. Truly an awful place—a place where any degree of warmth is excusable, and where coldness is not only unjustifiable but horrible. "I love those that thunder out the Word," said Whitefield. "The Christian world is in a deep sleep. Nothing but a loud voice can awaken them out of it."

can have any quietness in your minds; how you can eat or drink or rest till you have got some ground of everlasting consolations!

"Is that a man or a corpse that is not affected with matters of this importance? that can be readier to sleep than to tremble when he heareth how he must stand at the bar of God? Is that a man or a clod of clay that can rise or lie down without being deeply affected with his everlasting estate? that can follow his worldly business but make nothing of the great business of salvation or damnation; and that, when they know it is hard at hand? Truly, Sirs, when I think of the weight of the matter, I wonder at the very best of God's saints upon earth, that they are no better, and do no more in so weighty a case. I wonder at those whom the world accounteth more holy than necessary, and scorns for making too much ado, that they can put off Christ and their souls with so little; that they pour not out their souls in every supplication; that they are not more taken up with God; that their thoughts are not more serious in preparation of their accounts. I wonder that they be not an hundred times more strict in their lives, and more laborious and unwearied in striving for the crown than they are.

"Ready to Tremble"

"And for myself, as I am ashamed of my dull and careless heart, and of my slow and unprofitable course of life; so, the Lord knows, I am ashamed of every sermon I preach; when I think what I have been speaking of, and who sent me, and that men's salvation or damnation is so much concerned in it, I am ready to tremble lest God should judge me as a slighter of His truths and the souls of men, and lest in the best sermon I should be guilty of their blood. Methinks we should not speak a word to men in matters of such consequence without tears, or the greatest earnestness that possibly we can; were not we too much guilty of the sin which we reprove, it would be so."

We are not in *earnest* either in preaching or in hearing. If we were, could we be so cold, so prayerless, so inconsistent, so slothful, so worldly, so unlike men whose business is all about eternity? We must be more in earnest if we would win souls. We must be more in earnest if we would walk in the footsteps of our beloved Lord, or if we would fulfill the vows that are upon us. We must be more in earnest if we would be less than hypocrites. We must be more in earnest if we would finish our course with joy, and obtain the crown at the Master's coming. We must work while it is day; *the night cometh when no man can work.*